EXTREME HABITATS

MOUNTAINS

EMILY KINGTON

www.hungrytomato.com

First published by
Hungry Tomato Ltd in 2021,
F1, Old Bakery Studios,
Blewetts Wharf, Malpas Road,
Truro, Cornwall, TR1 1QH, UK

ISBN 978 1 914087 08 0

Manufactured in the USA

A CIP catalogue record for this book is available from the British Library.

Picture credits

(t = top, b = bottom, m = middle, l = left, r = right, bg = background)

Bryan Knox/Papilio/Corbis 21mr. Corbis Didrik Johnck/Corbis 9cr. Craig Lovell/Corbis 24tl. Jim Sugar/ Getty 16l. Karl Weatherly/Corbis 15bl. Luiz Claudio Marigo/naturepl.com 20tl. Marcos Delgado/epa/ Corbis 17tl. Shutterstock:4tl; 5mr; 6tl; 6bl; 8tl; 9bl; 10tl; 10b; 11tl; 12tl; 13br; 14t; 15mr; 21tr; 21br; 25br; 27br;Alan Freed 17mr; Andrij Vatsyk (front cover); Bruce Yeung 25mr; Cezary Wojtkowski 11br; Denis Pepin 26tl; Dmitry Pichugin 28bl; ene 21bl; Gaurav Aryal 1bg; Grigory Kubatyan 23br; Jakub Cejpek 7mr; James BO Insogna 13mr; Kondrachov Vladimir 20bl; kram-9 29bl; littlesam 18bg; LYA GENKIN 18bl; Maxim Petrichuk 27mr (mountain bike); Mike Laptev 2bg; moosehenderson 22tl; namonic 5b (hat); Nigel Paul Monckton 19mr; Paul Clarke 25tr; Paul Clarke 29br; Phawat 11mr; rangsan paidaen (fact file); Sharon Lumpkin 23mr; sinoptic (notebook and tips illustrations); Steven Bourelle 22bl; Styve Reineck 23tr; Svetlana Larina 27tr; Thomas Riggins 13tl; Vitalii Matokha 14bg; Vitalii Nesterchuk 7bl; Vixit 8bg; worker 26br; Wuttipong Potawin 4bg. Ulrich Doering/Alamy 24br. Wally McNamee/Corbis 27mr (bobsleigh).

Every effort has been made to trace the copyright holders, and we apologise in advance for any unintentional omissions. We would be pleased to insert the appropriate acknowledgements in any subsequent edition of this publication.

CONTENTS

WHAT IS A MOUNTAIN?

Map showing some of the world's most important mountains and mountain ranges.

Mountains are gigantic masses of rock with steep slopes, much higher than the land around them. Many mountains together can form a range so huge it affects the weather across entire continents.

Mountains are created over millions of years by immense forces under the ground. The Earth's **crust** is made up of huge slabs called plates, which fit together like a jigsaw puzzle. When **plates** collide, the land can be pushed upwards, forming mountains.

On their lower **slopes**, mountains are covered with trees and plants. Higher up, even in hot countries, they are covered with snow all year. This is because the higher above **sea level** you are, the colder it becomes. In this way, the **foothills** of a mountain may have a tropical climate, while the peak is icy cold.

Most mountains form a pointed peak because they get worn away by the weather. Water enters cracks in the rocks and freezes. This causes rocks to crack and come away from the mountain.

MOUNTAIN NOTEBOOK

- Mountains cover about a quarter of the Earth's surface, and they're found in 75 percent of countries.

MOUNTAINS IN HAWAII.

- Mountains influence rainfall. On Big Island in Hawaii, mountains block rainclouds from traveling southwest. The northeast part of the island has 10 feet (3 meters) of rain per year, while the southwest has just 30 inches (75 centimeters).

MOUNTAIN SURVIVAL TIPS

Hypothermia can occur when a body's temperature drops too low. You need to wear warm clothing on all parts of your body, it is vital to keep your body heat in.

Crampons are shoes with metal spikes at the bottom. They fit over climbing boots. They help climbers to grip the ice and hard snow.

JOURNEY TO THE TOP OF THE WORLD

Although they are breathtaking to look at, mountains can be dangerous to climb. If you want to get to the top of the highest mountains you must be fit, and have had the proper training. It's also important to take the right equipment.

There are two main dangers when climbing mountains: you could fall off into a **crevasse**; or things, such as rocks and ice, could fall on you.

For some people, like those in **mountain rescue teams**, climbing mountains is part of their job, and for others, it's just for fun.

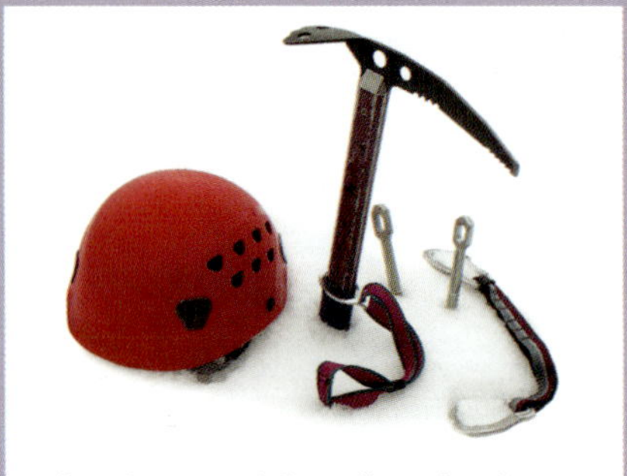

Safety is essential – take a hard helmet, ice axe and clips for climbing.

MOUNTAIN SURVIVAL TIPS

Dehydration can be a real problem on mountains, so melt plenty of snow for drinking water. Bring tablets to purify the water and enough fuel for your stove.

To climb mountains, you must be well equipped. Everything you take up, you must bring down – there are no bins on mountain tops and nobody will collect your rubbish.

Things that can fall on you include rocks, ice, snow, other climbers or their equipment. There are also dangers from unpredictable and harsh weather.

MOUNTAIN EQUIPMENT

- Ropes, clamps and other mountaineering equipment
- Ice axe
- Lots of layers of warm, lightweight clothing
- Sturdy boots
- Helmet and head torch
- Several pairs of gloves
- Sunscreen and lipsalve
- Goggles
- Two-way radio and satellite phone

BRIGHTLY COLORED TENTS ARE EASY TO SEE IN THE SNOW.

- Tent
- Sleeping bag
- Small stove, gas-based fuel and cooking equipment
- Food supplies (high energy, quick-cook food)
- Sack for collecting snow and ice, for melting
- Air tanks of bottled oxygen

THE HIGHEST PLACE ON EARTH

Prayer flags flying at a camp on Mount Everest. Local people believe the wind carries their prayers to the gods.

The highest mountain in the world is Mount Everest, at 29,000 feet (8,850 meters) above sea level. There is another mountain that is actually taller than Everest – Mauna Kea in Hawaii – but only 13,800 feet (4,207 meters) of it is above the sea.

Mount Everest is in the **Himalayan** mountain range of southern Asia on the border between Nepal and China.

MOUNTAIN SURVIVAL TIPS

Above 24,600 feet (7,500 meters), low oxygen levels can cause extreme tiredness, headaches and confusion. Take bottled oxygen if you plan to climb above this height.

Every year hundreds of people try to climb Everest. Nearly 6,000 people have reached the top, but over 300 climbers have never returned.

Mountain climbing requires more than physical strength. Could you cope with the long, exhausting days, the strong winds and the freezing cold?

Most expeditions climb the lower slopes of Mount Everest slowly, spending weeks getting used to the low oxygen levels at high **altitudes**. Above 26,247 feet (8,000 meters), oxygen levels are so low that people can not survive for long without using bottled oxygen tanks.

The highest slopes on Everest are almost lifeless. There are no plants above about 20,000 feet (6,000 meters).

MOUNTAIN NOTEBOOK

- The world's tallest skyscraper is Burj Khalifa, in Dubai, which is 2,717 feet (828 meters) tall. Everest is over 10 times higher than that.
- Everest is still growing by about 0.2 inches (5 millimeters) a year!

ABOVE 26,000 FEET (8,000 METERS), OXYGEN MASKS ARE USED ALL THE TIME, EVEN WHEN THE CLIMBERS ARE RELAXING.

- Only people in groups are allowed to climb Everest. No one goes alone. The average cost to join a group is around $45,000. This pays for the guides, insurance, equipment, food and a permit to climb.

People wishing to climb Mount Everest get experience by climbing smaller mountains first.

Farmers high up in the Andes raise llamas for their wool.

THE LONGEST RANGE

Some mountains are single peaks, but most are formed in ranges. Mountain ranges can run for hundreds of miles. The world's longest mountain range is the mid-Atlantic ridge, which runs for nearly 2,000 miles (16,000 kilometers) beneath the Atlantic Ocean.

On land, the longest mountain **range** is the **Andes**, which stretches across seven South American countries. It is about 4,500 miles (7,250 kilometers) long and up to 310 miles (500 kilometers) wide. The average height of the Andes is about 13,000 feet (4,000 meters).

Machu Picchu in Peru is the site of an ancient Inca ruin. It is about 8,000 feet (2,430 meters) high in the Andes, and is visited by thousands of tourists every year.

The Perito Moreno glacier lies between Chile and Argentina at the southern end of the Andes.

The Andes run north to the warm **Equator**, and south towards the bottom of South America. Its tallest mountain is Aconcagua in Argentina, which is 22,838 feet (6,961 meters) high. Most of the highest mountains in the Andes are **volcanoes**. Cotopaxi in Ecuador is one of the highest active volcanoes in the world. It is 19,347 feet (5,897 meters) tall.

The north of the Andes are close to the Equator, and the lower slopes have a humid, rainy climate. At their southern end, the Andes mountains are nearer to the **Antarctic** where it is much colder.

MOUNTAIN NOTEBOOK

- The Andes Mountains are so high that they can block winds and rain clouds. Some mountains have east slopes that are covered in rainforests, while the west slopes are dry, desert land.

GOLD IS FOUND THROUGHOUT THE ANDES.

- Some of the **minerals** found in the Andes include gold, silver, tin, copper, platinum, lead and zinc.

MOUNTAIN SURVIVAL TIPS

Frostbite occurs when extreme cold damages your skin and it becomes black and swollen. Protect your ears, nose, fingers, toes and cheeks.

The South American condor lives in the Andes. Its outstretched wings can measure 10 feet (3 meters) across.

A sudden snowstorm hits the Sierra Nevada mountains in the USA.

THE WORST WEATHER

As you climb higher up a mountain, the temperature drops, and strong winds make it feel even colder. Gales and blizzards make travel difficult and dangerous. Mountain climbers watch the weather carefully. They must change their plans if the conditions become too dangerous.

Weather changes on mountains are often sudden. Within minutes, a bright sunny day can change to freezing cold rain. Blizzards are particularly dangerous because the driving snow makes it hard for mountain climbers to see where they are going.

On Mount Everest there are only about two **weather windows**. These are periods of four or five days during the spring, when it's possible to climb the mountain with less chance of dangerous weather.

Even in bright sunshine, the temperature on Mount Everest is well below freezing. Climbers cover up as much as possible.

Buildings on Mount Rainier in Washington, USA, must be able to withstand heavy snowfall.

Mount McKinley in Alaska, USA is one of the coldest mountains on Earth. The average minimum temperature in January is –5.8 °F (–21 °C). It's the highest peak in North America and it's also a dangerous mountain to climb.

MOUNTAIN NOTEBOOK

- Wind rushes up mountains during the day, and down during the night.
- More mountain climbers die from being battered by blizzards than by falling.

LIGHTNING STRIKING MOUNTAINS.

- Lightning will tend to strike the highest point in an area, so it can be especially dangerous on mountains.

MOUNTAIN SURVIVAL TIPS

Wear goggles to avoid snowblindness, which is like sunburn to your eyes. It is caused by bright sunlight reflected from the snow and ice.

Mount McKinley in Alaska, USA.

THE MOST DANGEROUS TO CLIMB

The Himalayan mountain range.

K2 in the Himalayas is 28,251 feet (8,611 meters) tall, the second highest mountain in the world. It is considered to be one of the most difficult mountains to climb. Although it's not as tall as Everest, the climbing conditions on K2 are far harder.

Above 20,000 feet (6,000 meters), K2 is blanketed with thick snow and ice. Less than 400 people have climbed to the top.

K2 has none of the **weather windows** that **Mount Everest** has, so it's almost impossible to climb without being caught in life-threatening weather.

Another reason why K2 is so dangerous is the steepness of its slopes. Climbers need special mountaineering equipment, and **avalanches** are common.

MOUNTAIN SURVIVAL TIPS

Before climbing any mountain, check to see if the conditions make avalanches likely. Always climb in a group. You must be prepared to dig each other out if an avalanche does occur.

Mountain climbers are roped together for safety.

MOUNTAIN NOTEBOOK

- Avalanches can be triggered by natural events or accidentally by humans.

ALL MEMBERS OF A TEAM SHOULD CARRY AN AVALANCHE RESCUE BEACON.

- An avalanche rescue beacon transmits a 'send' signal. If an avalanche buries some members of the group, the others switch their beacons to 'receive'. They can pick up the 'send' signals of the victims, and work quickly to dig them out.

If you're buried in snow from an avalanche, your rescuers will need to act fast. The weight of the heavy snow will make it hard to breathe.

DEADLY MOUNTAINS

If all the other risks when climbing mountains weren't enough, there are also dangers from volcanoes, flash floods and landslides.

Volcanoes are openings in the Earth's crust, and they are the deadliest mountains of all. An erupting volcano can send fiery clouds of hot ash, gas and red-hot liquid rock into the sky. The liquid rock, called **lava**, flows down the mountain at temperatures of up to 2,190°F (1,200°C).

International scientists watch about 24 volcanoes very closely. These volcanoes are dangerous because they have a high risk of erupting, and many people live close to them. They include Mount Rainier in the United States and Mount Etna in Italy.

MOUNTAIN SURVIVAL TIPS

People live close to volcanoes because the soil near volcanoes is rich and fertile – good for growing crops and grazing animals.

A mud landslide has run down the slopes of a mountain in Guatemala and buried the village at the bottom.

MOUNTAIN NOTEBOOK

- Mount Erebus is the largest volcano in Antarctica. It is 12,448 feet (3,794 meters) high, and it frequently spurts out sprays of hot lava.

MOUNT VESUVIUS HAS BEEN QUIET SINCE 1944, BUT IT COULD ERUPT WITH LITTLE WARNING.

- If Mount Vesuvius in Italy were to errupt again, it could destroy the entire city of Naples.

Landslides can be particularly devastating on mountains without forests on their lower slopes. Without the forest to soak up rainfall and the strong network of roots, soil is washed away in huge mud rivers which damage everything in their path.

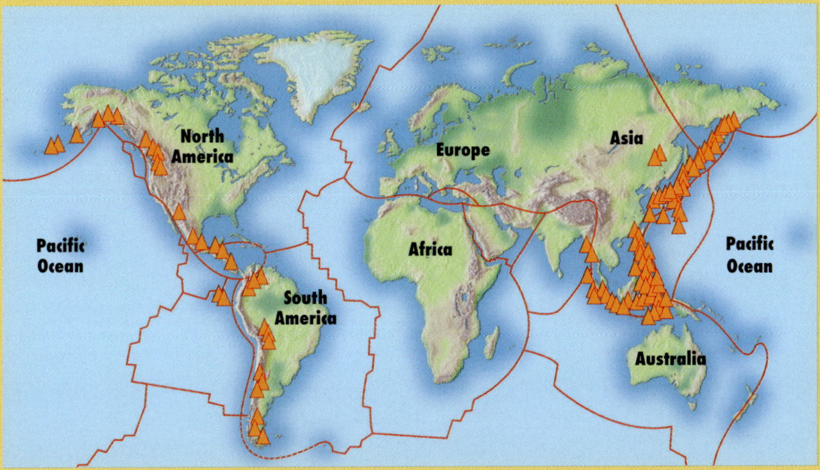

The orange triangles on the map show active volcanoes around the Pacific Ocean. This area is known as the 'Ring of Fire'. Volcanoes are usually found at plate boundaries, which are also marked on the map as red lines.

MAJESTIC MOUNTAINS

High peaks are majestic and awesome, and they often inspire a sense of wonder in the people that see them. This is why so many people want to climb tall mountains, despite the dangers.

Some mountains are considered **sacred**. Mount Fuji, in Japan, is one such mountain. More than 200,000 people climb to the top each year to pray. Most people climb Mount Fuji in two days, staying overnight in special mountain huts.

The Three Sisters are three huge pillars of rock. They are found in the Blue Mountains in Australia.

Most countries are proud of their mountains. Many mountain areas have been turned into national parks to protect them. The **Blue Mountains** near Sydney in Australia are a national park. These enormous cliffs have dramatic rock formations. They got their name because oil evaporating from eucalyptus trees creates a blue haze.

Mount Fuji is Japan's tallest mountain, at 12,389 feet (3,776 meters), and is known for its beautiful shape. Although Mount Fuji is a volcano, there is little danger of it erupting today.

MOUNTAIN NOTEBOOK

- Mount Kilimanjaro in Tanzania is the highest mountain in Africa. It is also the world's highest mountain that is not part of a mountain range.

TABLE MOUNTAIN, SOUTH AFRICA

- Table Mountain in South Africa was named because its summit is as flat as a table top. It is often covered in clouds, which people call the 'tablecloth'.

MOUNTAIN SURVIVAL TIPS

Mountain streams and melted snow can contain bacteria, so purify your water before you drink it. Use water purifying tablets that are fit for this purpose.

FACT FILE:

PLANT SURVIVORS

The puya lives for up to 150 years. It has the tallest flower of any plant.

The giant groundsel plant in Africa uses its dead leaves to protect its stem from the cold.

Plants can't live without water and minerals. They can't move around to find what they need, and they can't run from danger. It's difficult for plants to survive in icy temperatures and biting winds, so mountain plants have special adaptations.

- The two biggest problems mountain plants face are low temperatures and the lack of water.
- Some plants keep warm with a furry or hairy covering on leaves and stems. The puya of the Andes protects its giant flower spike with a prickly covering.
- Hairy plants are also protected from the Sun's damaging **ultraviolet** rays, which are stronger at high altitudes than anywhere else.
- Some plants have **waxy** leaves to reduce water loss, some have extra absorbent leaves or roots that take in whatever water they can find.
- Some plants have special **sap** to prevent their cells from freezing solid.

MOUNTAIN PLANTS

Edelweiss

- In the European Alps, tiny Edelweiss plants grow in cracks in rocks.
- Their waxy leaves retain any water and hairy stems and leaves keep them warm.

Edelweiss

Alpine snowbell

- The alpine snowbell pushes its new shoots through the snow each spring, giving off enough heat to melt the ice!
- Its petals vary from blue to purple depending on the habitat.

Alpine snowbell

Diapensia

- Several mountain plants, such as diapensia, remain small, huddled together in low mounds of tightly packed leaves.
- Staying close to the ground protects them from freezing winds.

Diapensia

Plants must also protect themselves from being eaten by grazing mountain animals. The wild nettle of the Andes does this with its very spiky leaves.

This chart shows the different altitudes at which plants live on some mountains.

ALTITUDE	PLANT
3,500 FEET	BROAD LEAFED TREES
6,500 FEET	CONIFER TREES
10,000 FEET	SHRUBS
11,000 FEET	ALPINE FLOWERS
13,000 FEET	LICHEN

FACT FILE

MOUNTAIN LIONS LIVE IN THE ROCKY MOUNTAINS, IN THE USA.

ANIMAL SURVIVORS

You might think that no animal could cope with the dreadful weather and steep and slippery slopes of mountains, but several do. Many animals have special adaptations to mountains, such as warm, thick fur coats.

- The mountain goat lives only in North America. It is often found at altitudes as high as 10,000 feet (3,000 meters).
- Mountain animals are usually agile and sure-footed. Most can run along steep slopes with ease.

The bald eagle lives on mountains throughout North America.

- Food is scarce, so only a few **predators** can survive on any mountain. These include snow leopards in the Himalayas, mountain lions in parts of the Rocky Mountains and timber wolves and lynxes on the mountains of Alaska.
- Only powerful birds can withstand the strong mountain winds. They include eagles, falcons and the Andean condor. These birds feed on small mountain mammals.

MOUNTAIN SURVIVORS

Mountain gorilla

- There are just over 1,000 mountain gorillas left, but conservation work is helping to increase their population again.
- They live on high slopes in central Africa.
- Their fur is longer than other gorillas, to protect them from the cold.

Mountain gorilla

Bighorn sheep

- These sheep live in the Rocky Mountains. They have good eyesight and hearing to alert them to danger.
- They eat large amounts of grass and then go to narrow ledges to digest it. While they are digesting their food, they are safe from predators.

Bighorn sheep

Guanaco

- Guanacos are part of the camel family, but they do not have humps. They have thick coats of long wool for warmth.
- They are expert browsers, finding plenty of food in the scrubby grasslands of the Andes.

Guanaco

MOUNTAIN GOAT ADAPTATIONS

FACT FILE

About 45 percent of the people of Bolivia live at altitudes above 20,000 feet (3,000 meters).

MOUNTAIN PEOPLE

People who live near sea level often feel dizzy or short of breath if they climb above 20,000 feet (3,000 meters). Yet many people live comfortably in towns along mountain ranges. La Paz, the capital of Bolivia, is 11,800 feet (3,600 meters) above sea level and the town of Wenzhuan in the Himalayas is 16,700 feet (5,100 meters).

- The Quechua people live high up in the Andes. They have bigger hearts and lungs than most people to carry more oxygen to their blood.
- The Quechua people have extra **blood vessels** in their feet to keep them warmer.
- Across parts of northern China, millions of people make their homes in mountain caves called yaodongs. Yaodong means 'arched tunnel' in Chinese. The mountain **insulates** the caves, keeping them warm in winter and cool in summer.
- Today, some **Sherpa** people make their living guiding tourists up the high mountains of the Himalayas.

The Sherpa people use dzos for ploughing their farmland. A dzo is a cross between a yak and a cow.

FACT FILE

This is a list of some of the highest towns in different countries around the world.

TOWN	COUNTRY	CONTINENT	ALTITUDE
WENZHUAN	TIBET	ASIA	16,730 FEET
LA RICONADA	PERU	SOUTH AMERICA	16,730 FEET
GAITE	INDIA	ASIA	14,440 FEET
DOLPA	NEPAL	ASIA	14,300 FEET
EL ALTO	BOLIVIA	SOUTH AMERICA	13,450 FEET
APARTADEROS	VENEZUELA	SOUTH AMERICA	11,500 FEET
LEADVILLE	UNITED STATES	NORTH AMERICA	10,430 FEET
QUITO	ECUADOR	SOUTH AMERICA	9,350 FEET
KURUSH	RUSSIA	ASIA	8,140 FEET
EL SERRAT	ANDORRA	EUROPE	7,770 FEET

AROUND THE WORLD

Bolivia, South America

- The Aymara people live around Lake Titicaca in the Andes Mountains, the highest lake in South America.
- They use rafts and small rowing boats to catch the fish in the lake.

Fishing boat on Lake Titicaca

Nepal, Asia

- Farmers in some parts of Nepal cut giant steps into the hillside and build walls round them to hold in soil and water.
- They grow potatoes, rice, wheat, barley and apricots in these fields.

Sherpa farm

Tanzania, Africa

- People of the Chagga tribe live on the southern and eastern slopes of Mount Kilimanjaro and Mount Meru.
- Their main crops are coffee and bananas.

A Chagga woman carries bananas

FACT FILE

Skiing is a very popular sport. About 120 million tourists visit the European Alps each year.

MOUNTAINS TODAY

The high slopes of most mountains in the world have been left in their natural state. They are mainly used for recreation. People travel all over the world in search of the perfect mountain for hiking, cycling, skiing or snowboarding.

- Mountain **tourism** has grown and people visit mountains to try out sports, breathe in the clearer air, or to enjoy the spectacular views.
- Skiing is a traditional mountain sport. Most mountain sports feature speed and danger and require lots of specialized equipment.
- The coffee plant grows best in tropical mountains. The best quality coffee comes from bushes that are at altitudes above 3280 feet (1,000 meters) – although not in areas that receive any frost.
- Plants that can be used to make medicines are found on many mountains of the world, such as the Himalayas and the Alps.
- Almost all medicinal mountain plants are collected from the wild. They are not farmed like other crops.

The coffee grown in the Blue Mountains in Jamaica is considered to be some of the best tasting in the world.

FACT FILE

MOUNTAIN SPORTS

Snowboarding

- A cross between skiing and skateboarding.
- In downhill snowboarding, the aim is to get to the bottom of the mountain as quickly as possible.
- In freestyle snowboarding, the stunts and jumps are more important.

Bobsleighing

- Sleighs run down an icy track with many bends in it.
- Teams compete to see who can go the fastest.

Mountain Biking

- Riders must be able to power their bikes up steep hills and control them down sheer slopes.
- Mountain bikes have extra suspension, lots of gears and thick tires with many bumps to help grip the surface.

Snowboarding

Bobsleigh

Mountain biking

This chart shows some of the mountain plants used in traditional medicines.

PLANT	FOUND IN	HELPS TREAT
BARBERRY	HIMALAYAS	EYE DISEASES
GENTIANS	ANDES	LIVER PROBLEMS
HIMALAYAN YEW	HIMALAYAS	CANCER
PERUVIAN BARK	ANDES	MALARIA
SNOW LOTUS	HIMALAYAS	RHEUMATISM
SWERTIA	HIMALAYAS	HEART PROBLEMS

The bark of the barberry plant is used to treat sore eyes and fevers.

FACT FILE

MOUNTAINS IN DANGER

Mountain habitats are more fragile than they look. Some problems are caused by the people who live there, particularly the poorest people, who may need to cut down trees for firewood. Other damage is caused by tourists who visit the mountains.

- Some native mountain people cut down forests for firewood. With fewer trees, the rain washes away the soil. This silts up rivers, which can cause a shortage of water further down the mountain.
- Climbers have dumped tons of rubbish on Mount Everest, including cans, plastic containers, glass, clothes and tents.
- Nepal army helicopters are being used to lift some of the waste.
- Thankfully, most people who visit mountains treat the unique environment with respect. They follow the saying "take only pictures, leave only footprints".

This mountain in Nepal has been nicknamed 'Fishtail' because its top looks like a fish's tail. It is a sacred mountain, and climbers are not allowed up it.

TYPES OF MOUNTAIN

People can have a big effect on the environment on the slopes of mountain, but there is very little we can do to the mountain itself. Mountains are usually formed over thousands of years, and we are not able to influence this process.

Fold mountains

- Movement of the Earth's plates can cause layers of rocks to push against each other.
- The rocks crumple and bulge. Mountains are pushed up and valleys are squeezed down.
- Most of the mountains in the Alps are fold mountains.

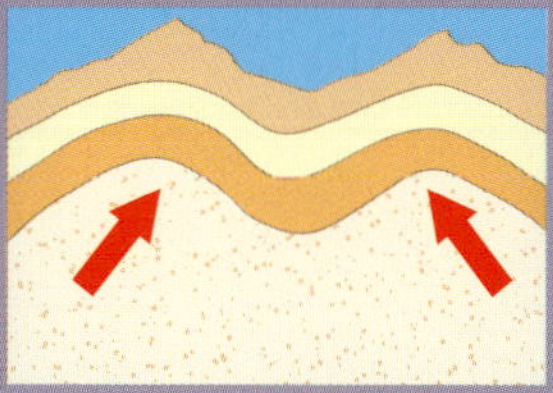

Fold mountain

Fault mountains

- The surface of the Earth sometimes cracks along a fault.
- Layers of rock on one side of the crack can be pushed up to form a mountain.

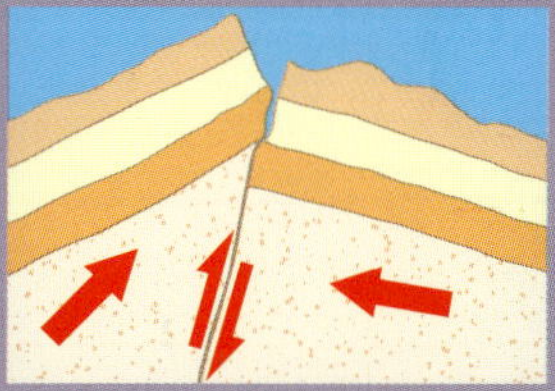

Fault mountain

Volcanic mountains

- When a volcano erupts, it pushes out lava.
- The lava hardens and cools, sometimes forming a mountain.
- Mount Fuji and Mount Vesuvius are examples of volcanic mountains.

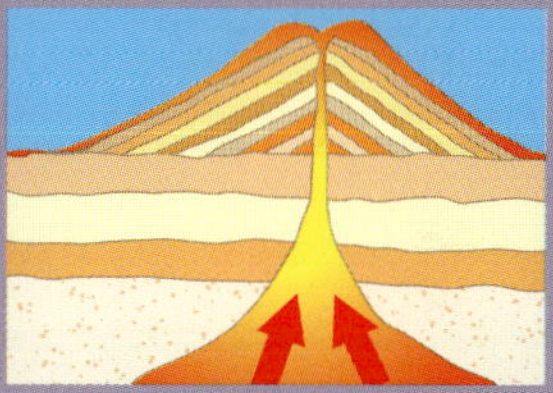

Volcanic mountain

People are beginning to realize the dangers of cutting down the mountain forests, and they are now planting new trees.

Only 500 people a day are allowed to walk the Inca Trail in Peru. This is to protect the vulnerable mountain path.

GLOSSARY

Alps – a mountain range in Southern Europe.

altitude – the height of an object above a given point, such as sea level.

Andes – the world's longest mountain range, stretching about 4,500 miles (7,250 kilometers) down the western coast of South America.

Antarctic – the land surrounding the South Pole.

avalanches – sliding masses of snow and ice that can move at speeds of more than 1.2 miles (2 kilometers) per minute.

blood vessels – tubes which carry blood around the body.

Blue Mountains –
1. A group of cliffs in southern Australia, about 3,280 feet (1,000 meters) high.
2. A mountainous region of Jamaica.

continents – the huge areas of land on Earth that each contain many countries. There are seven continents: Europe, North and South America, Africa, Australia, Asia and Antarctica.

crevasse – a deep crack in the ground.

crust – the outer layer of Earth.

Equator – an imaginary line around the Earth, dividing the world into a northern half and southern half.

fault – a crack in the Earth's crust, often where plates meet.

flash floods – sudden rushes of water after heavy rains.

foothills – low hills at the bottom of mountains.

glacier – a mass of ice and snow.

Himalayan – relating to the enormous mountain range stretching across southern Asia. Many of the world's highest mountains are here, including most of the peaks over 23,000 feet (7,000 meters).

hypothermia – when the body's temperature drops dangerously. It can cause a person to become unable to move properly or think clearly.

insulate – to protect something from heat or cold by covering it.

K2 – the world's second highest mountain, found on the borders of Pakistan and China in the Himalayas.

landslides – when earth and rocks fall down a mountain.

lava – hot, liquid rock.

Mauna Kea – the biggest mountain in the world, measured from its base to its top.

minerals – substances found in the ground, such as gold or tin.

Mount Everest – the world's highest mountain. It is 29,000 feet (8,850 meters) tall and is found on the borders of Nepal and China in the Himalayas.

Mount Kilimanjaro – the tallest mountain in Africa, and the tallest free standing mountain (not part of a mountain range) in the world. It is 19,341 feet (5,895 meters) tall and it is in Tanzania.

mountain rescue team – a team of people who look for climbers and hikers who have become lost on a mountain.

oxygen – a gas in the Earth's atmosphere, which animals need to breathe.

plates – the huge slabs below the Earth's crust which the land and oceans rest upon. These plates are moving slowly all the time.

predators – animals which catch other animals for food.

range – a group of mountains.

Rocky Mountains – the largest mountain range in North America, stretching 3000 miles (4,800 kilometers) along the western parts of Canada and the United States.

sacred – something or somewhere considered to be of religious or spiritual significance.

sap – the liquid part of a plant.

sea level – the sea's surface. It is used as a starting point for measuring the height of mountains and other objects.

Sherpa – a group of people from the Himalayan part of Nepal.

silt – tiny parts of earth that can block up a river and prevent it from flowing easily.

slopes – parts of the side of a mountain.

tourism – visits by holidaymakers to places of interest.

ultraviolet – the invisible light given off by the Sun. It can cause damage to plants, animals and people.

volcano – a mountain formed by lava which is forced up through a gap in the earth. Volcanoes often have a hollow top.

waxy – a waterproof covering resembling candle wax.

weather window – the good weather in between periods of storms. Climbers try to plan their trips in these windows.

INDEX